Dexter
the Shelter Dog

BY: TONI MARSH

AuthorHouse
1663 Liberty Drive
Bloomington, IN 47403
www.authorhouse.com
Phone: 1 (800) 839-8640

Published by AuthorHouse 09/26/2018

ISBN: 978-1-5462-6186-5 (sc)
ISBN: 978-1-5462-6185-8 (e)

Library of Congress Control Number: 2018911465

Print information available on the last page.

authorHOUSE®

Dexter the Shelter Dog

Toni Marsh

This book is for the little life
growing inside of me.
I can't wait to read to you.

Dexter the shelter dog wants to play outside today.

Patiently, he waits
his turn
for Annie the
animal caregiver

To pet his head
and leash him up
and take him
outside for a
walk.

Dexter the shelter dog gets sad after every walk

because play time is not long enough. Annie needs to care for every dog.

EVERY night when
he's asleep
he dreams to be
part of a family.

Dexter the shelter dog watches as people pass him by.

Suddenly, a girl appears and pets him softly behind the ears.

She asked, "would you like to come home with me?" Dexter started barking joyfully.

Dexter the adopted dog has his very own family and a home.

About the Author

Toni Marsh can warm the hearts of families everywhere with her inspirational book "Dexter the Shelter Dog". She can quickly capture your attention and bring long lasting joy to young readers.

Printed in the United States
By Bookmasters